Praise

"Recently, I watched *My Dinner with Andre*, a film I haven't seen in some forty years. Watching it again, I was struck by how the two speakers listen with such care to one another, responding, even when they disagree, with tenderness. That's what I feel while reading *Birds of Sympathy: Correspondences,* this conversation-in-poems between George Looney and Douglas Smith. Their interchange, as they probe 'the mystery / of what it means to be human,' feels intimate and always human. Smith writes, 'Every angel carries a miraculous message to us,' and readers will certainly find the miraculous in *Birds of Sympathy*. As well as language that, over and over, makes Rilke, and his terrible angels, swoon."

—John Bradley, author of *Hotel Montparnasse: Letters to César Vallejo*

"In *Birds of Sympathy,* poets George Looney and the late Douglas Smith record a yearslong dialogue of love and hurt and grace. It's a conversation that achieves intimacy and depth seldom reached for, even among lovers, much less friends. 'We always speak of loss when we speak of love,' a poem tells us, and it bears Smith's initials. There's pain in reading words from one who is lost to another who is left, their correspondence silenced. It's a bird that comes home to roost when Looney notes that 'every relationship is terminal,' a condition that separates us from indifferent angels and is 'the only thing that makes light possible.' When Smith closes a poem, 'Let me know if the light reaches you,' we feel it has, but it's the gold, end-of-day kind that rends what it illumines.

—Karen Craigo, former Poet Laureate of Missouri, author of *Passing Through Humansville*

Birds of Sympathy: Correspondences

Douglas Smith
George Looney

APRIL GLOAMING

Publisher's Cataloguing-in-Publication Data

Smith, Douglas & George Looney
   Birds of sympath: Correspondences / written by Douglas Smith &
   George Looney
   ISBN: 978-1-953932-14-3

1. Poetry: General 2. Poetry: American - General I. Title II. Author

Library of Congress Control Number: 2022951354

for the terrible angels

Contents

I lean back, as the evening darkens and comes on.
A chicken hawk floats over, looking for home.
I have wasted my life.
        —James Wright

I say let the corpse dance. Make the living lie still.
        —Richard Hugo

Spiraling Above Us

–Douglas Smith

When I think about our journey last summer,
I always remember the birds. I remember
the sad roadrunner by the shimmering highway,
waiting, watching, and sometimes I call the bird *Goyen*
and laugh. I remember the eloquent hawk
spiraling above us and the way its shadow slid
across the highway and splashed into the car.
I remember the brown jay with one leg,
how it followed us, hopping, and how
we fed it the next day when it landed on our table
during dinner. If we return to that distant state,
I hope we can find the birds, all the birds.

In Clouds of White Wings

–George Looney

Was it a roadrunner, or another sad bird
who, changed by its sorrow,
seemed to take up that name with such longing
it would have been a sin not to accept its pretense?
And what of the cattle egrets,
clouds of them lifting from the hillocks
and fields, and the occasional lone white bird
flying low along the horizon's curve
in that place not far from the weather of the ocean?
That brown jay exists in the amnesia of passion,
where it becomes a blessing, the best
any of us can hope to become. We must
learn to accept despair with grace,
like the cattle accept those startling birds.
Suffering may stand in fields inside us
like cattle in the fields in Texas, but there
is the possible miracle of egrets
lifting in clouds of white wings, the blessing
of one drifting on a current of air
like nothing so much as joy. Take as much
pleasure as you can in those you love,
and whatever birds may grace your landscape.

The Salt Water Bitter

–Douglas Smith

I remember our trip to the coast
with some pleasure and some sorrow.
We drove to the edge of the continent
and then walked into the cold water
until the water lifted us from the shifting
surface of earth, and then talked
while small silver fish rose from the waves
around us. We discussed many things,
but one subject shivered and moved through
all the others: passion. I knew then
how much you suffered, and I wanted to help,
but passion and suffering always swim together.
I know this is true, but I still tried
that day (the saltwater bitter in my eyes)
to bring some solace to your world.

Difficult to Believe

—George Looney

Solace is a fish that scuttles past the ankles
of men and women who venture from the plates
that hold up continents. Its fins touch flesh
like a friend's laugh about something painful.
You did bring solace, and I am more grateful
than something as clumsy as language
can express. As I'm grateful for the angel.
It can be difficult to believe in her, but I continue to
struggle, uncertain whether angels and men
can stay together, with or without going mad.
Be as comforted as any of us can be
who swim waters with such conflicting currents.

We Wait for the Holy

    −Douglas Smith

Angels and men cannot remain together
unless the angels become men
or the men become angels: that is the nature
of angels and men. *Every angel is terrible,*
Rilke said. Even if we cry out,
the angelic orders remain silent
and indifferent, and so we wait. We wait
for the holy and the human to merge.
I believe there's something sacred in each
human, but I also believe
a necessary transformation must occur:
although we can never arrive,
we must move toward the angelic orders.
Even if the angel rises away from us,
we should continue to move toward what is
sacred, for the journey will transform us.

To Love the Wound

—George Looney

Every angel *is* terrible, especially
those who offer the greatest grace.
Since when we can't rise to touch
(and be touched by) that grace,
the despair and the futility of being
only a man is all the more devastating.
Still, we must stand *on* the earth
and not turn a deaf ear to whatever choirs
(angelic or otherwise) may open their mouths
in song. The horizon is uncertain,
as it always is for men. Are angels certain
because the horizon doesn't matter to them?
Perhaps what you say is true about men
and angels, unless a man can learn to love
the wound reopened over and over
in his thigh. As Kinnell wrote, *it must be*
the wound, the wound itself, which
lets us know and love. I try to love
the wound in order to love the angel.
Perhaps that's the closest I'll come
to moving toward the sacred: hoping
the wound, by becoming me,
is the necessary transformation.
Is it madness to try to love the wound?
Or all we can do? May your wound be
only a scar—a memory of the wounding.

18

After the Losses

–Douglas Smith

Every angel carries a miraculous message to us,
and we spend our lives trying to decipher
the code. We want the message to transform us,
but we cannot know the language, and so a wound
rises through us. I agree the necessary wound
allows us to know and love, and hope
you remember that during this bleak time.
(*I know how furiously your heart is beating*,
Wallace Stevens said, and I can say the same.)
I also hope you will remember the following
passage from Andre Dubus's *Broken Vessels*:
So my crippling is a daily and living sculpture
of certain truths: we receive and we lose,
and we must try to achieve gratitude;
and with that gratitude to embrace with whole hearts
whatever of life that remains after the losses.
I believe such gratitude requires faith,
and faith is another name for love. We must believe
some miraculous figure moves beyond us
and toward us: if we cannot believe,
we cannot move through the remarkable world.
We always speak of loss when we speak of love.
We have no choice: the angel is the wound,
and the message is the dark scar we carry with us.
Louise Glück understands the inevitable
nature of the angelic wound: *Why love what you will*

lose?/There is nothing else to love.
We cannot avoid the wound, but faith
allows us to transform that dark mysterious scar
into the possibility of grace. We should
remember Stanley Plumly's idea: *Language is
a darkness pulled out of us.* We should
also embrace another idea: language is
a light that rises from the darkness
within us. I hope that this contains certain shards
of light. Let me know if the light reaches you.

Nothing Else to Love

−George Looney

Do we love only because of our knowledge
of the wound? Is the light by which we must see
the miraculous and mysterious figure
tinted with the darkness the wound reveals
within us? What message might be inscribed
on what is revealed by such light?
That there's nothing else to love but loss?
And what choir would we need to gather
to move an angel? Only language can sing
through the indifference of the angel.
But can the voice that sings come from
the wound? Can an angel point to
a map on a wall and guide us? Should we
deny the light because of the dark it carries
within it? And if we do, what's left?
Not even the dark is certain then. Or faith,
which allows us to transform the dark
into grace. We must discover a faith
we can hold with the image of the angel
standing in front of us, or the wound
will overwhelm light and the dark will be all words
can form, no figure and no map on any wall
offering any direction at all. Still, I'm not
completely lost. I know this must head south
to find you, with the steady light, I pray, of
your own miraculous figure surrounding you.

My Good Dream and My Agony

–Douglas Smith

We want to live in a world of mystery and passion,
where angels fall and gods rise within us.
We cannot live without the possibility of grace
and beauty and order. We have to invent
(in the absence of angels) a new world
of revelations to embrace. Sometimes our desire
to create this new world, this different life,
leads us toward a pattern of darkness,
for the imaginary landscape we invent refuses
to rise into the true world. Wendell Berry
certainly understands this pattern
of darkness: *What the world could be*
is my good dream and my agony
when, dreaming it, I lie awake and turn
and look into the dark. Although we may
fail again and again, we must continue to
invent new worlds, new stories,
or we will allow the dark wound to cover us.
Sometimes we have to invent light in order
to walk through darkness. We have to remember
Wendell Berry's words: *Practice resurrection.*

The Angel in Absentia

–George Looney

We want there to be a map to the world
that is a wound. We want an angel
to guide us in the absence of such a map.
We want too much what we cannot have,
and the wound rises like a god within us
and blocks what raspy songs an angel
might send us as guide. *Practice resurrection?*
Perhaps Wendell Berry's right. That is
what we do in the histories of our wounds.
Wondering, each time we limp back
to the passion, why we're drawn
toward a false light full of pain that enters
our wound and pulls the wound with it
so the wound becomes the guide, the angel
in absentia. No god rises *in* a wound;
gods rise *from* wounds. And no wound
can be, as Wendell Berry says, the *grace*
of necessary things; no wound can *heal*
the earth, and heal men. Once we have
arrived at this, what can be a poultice
for the pain (and pleasure) it took to get there?
And how do we deny the wound that *is*
understanding? The only light I can see
or invent is the light I know is temporary,
that is the wound itself. I don't know
how to get past the pain, or see or invent

what could be beyond it. I can't see
past the wound, and the only chance
for healing is for me to invent it.
This, then, is a dispatch from despair.

Composed of Contrary Things

–Douglas Smith

There are seasons of jagged darkness
in human life, but there are also moments
of grace and light and beauty,
and we should embrace those when the night
is too much with us. Montaigne would
agree: *We must learn to endure
what we cannot avoid. Our life is
composed, like the harmony of the world,
of contrary things, also of different tones,
sweet and harsh, sharp and flat, soft
and loud. If a musician liked only one kind,
what would he have to say?* We must
not allow darkness to overwhelm us,
for then we are alone and without hope,
and we cannot invent a world to live in
without hope. Listen to Lewis Thomas
speak about the possibility of hope: *The good
thought I have about this is that we are,
to begin with, the most improbable of all
the earth's creatures, and maybe
it is not beyond hope that we are also endowed
with improbable luck.* We are improbable
creatures, my friend, but not beyond
hope. Something to remember in the night.

The Music Still Left

—George Looney

Sometimes we come to the point in this
dream of pain and sorrow
the angels offer us as consolation
for the bodies we live in that we must,
as Montaigne said, *learn to endure
what we cannot avoid.* Knowledge
of loss, for example. Is such knowing
itself an angel, perhaps the very one loosed
from me, that I've wanted to hold
and be consumed in the light of? I must
find ways to listen to the music
still left in my poor body—the fugue
we call memory—and not tear at
my own flesh to rip out whatever organ
plays it over and over. Memory
is an angel, and Rilke was right. Every angel
is terrible. And I am a bitter,
improbable creature not endowed with luck.
Though angels are terrible, all I want is
to embrace one angel, endure one terror.

The Mouth of a Labyrinth

–Douglas Smith

The asylum of memory allows us to endure.
When we leave the asylum,
we enter a strange world of terrible beauty.
*The beauty of the world is the mouth
of a labyrinth,* Simone Weil said,
but if we emerge from the labyrinth, we have
another vision to carry with us.
We must sing the fugue we call memory:
we are singers at large, and we do not belong.
Even if the angel rises away from us,
we must sing. Even if the father
slides into dark water, we must sing.
We have no choice: even when affliction
threatens to engulf us, we must
remember the beauty and mystery of the world
we live in, and we must sing.
Without memory, we will disappear,
so we must return to that asylum and sing
of passion and anguish. Consider this
a dispatch from one asylum to another.

The Voices We Give Them

–George Looney

Memory *is* an asylum. And the attendants are angels.
The halls of the asylum echo with screams
from behind locked doors, each scream an echo
of *ekstasis*. It's no accident the root word for ecstasy
means *terror*. In one room, St. Therese is still rising,
still feeling the draw of flesh, the flapping of wings
and the surging of blood. Every angel *is* terrible.
They work us over behind locked doors, as if torture
were the only hope for us. And the days
our attendants don't torture us, when our angels are
absent, make us want to believe, as Eluard said,
that *forgetfulness is useful for the preservation
of the individual.* But in our locked rooms,
that's not what we want to be, not the desire
of memory, which insists we are not individual,
but many and varied. And in flux, always.
The attendants whisper through the doors at night,
their voices the voices we give them, speaking
of tenderness and joy, all the lies
we would have them say while they work us over
with whatever we've dreamed up for them to
hurt us with. The asylum of memory fills
with our screaming and cursing and whimpering.
Or whispering gently through locked doors.
It's no place to live. It may be the only place
we *do* live. I hope the whispers through your door

comfort you. That they have a real body forming them,
that they're not the voice of some troubled ghost.

In the Absence of Evidence

–Douglas Smith

We desire the condition of faith. We want
to believe something will happen to us,
that some miracle will transform the world
we live in. We want to believe
that passion and beauty and tenderness
can still exist in the true and dark world.
We must continue to have faith,
even in the absence of evidence.
There is no way to ease the burden,
Donald Justice said, but we must not
accept this: we are with Jacob by the river
at night, and we must struggle to rise
until the light appears. When we finally rise
and limp away, we will know
the quality of darkness, but
we will also know the glory of light.
We should remember that glory,
and we should praise it. *The art of losing*
isn't hard to master, Elizabeth Bishop
said. Please consider me
with you in the practice of that art.

Like a Leper, Limping

—George Looney

In Hugo's *Death and the Good Life*,
Al "Mush Heart" Barnes, says,
I thought of a world where life is
always too hard, where we are asked
to endure more than we can
ever really bear. I bawled like a baby
for no one in particular and for all of us.
Mush Heart was bawling for everyone
forced to master the art of losing.
How much can we endure, and believe in
passion and beauty and tenderness? The world,
Hugo knew, can be cold and numb.
Which is why he loved Ripley so much
those late years. But Ripley was no angel.
She was a woman, a good woman.
And that's the trick. To love a good woman
makes tenderness and passion possible.
Trying to love an angel wrapped away from
the world in layers of indifference
leads to madness. I've asked if it was madness
to try to love the wound. (Even back then,
Jacob had entered this conversation,
moving through these letters like a leper,
limping more and more.) It *is* madness.
No one should have to love a wound.
Justice may have been right. Perhaps

there's no way to ease the burden. So how
do we bear it? Why do we hold onto
passion when to do so is madness? Why
do we hold on even as bruises flower
over our flesh from the blows? Why
is it so difficult to let go of passion,
of hope? Maybe because it *is* passion.
It *is* hope. And without these, what are we?
We are not angels. We must not be
indifferent. We must struggle to hold the angel
all night beside a dark river. As long
as the river and the night last. As long
as we believe the angel wants to be human.
But when the angel is so distant
passion is a memory, when she embraces
Misery, the river that sings her name,
we must walk away from that river's bank
in gray light, limping to some place
we can't see on the horizon where
the wound becomes a scar, a pale reminder
in flesh, where we can sing our praises
to something other than the pain
we must not embrace, the wound
it would be madness to try to love.

Toward Something We Cannot Name

—Douglas Smith

I still believe the shimmering mystery of language
can redeem the difficult and broken landscapes
we live in. When the ancient stories fail
to console us at night, I believe we should relish
the miraculous gift of language
to shape new landscapes and new stories.
Consider the strange nature of language,
the way it roams beyond where we want to go,
beyond what we want to see. Consider
the way language moves us toward something
we cannot name. *Every word was once
an animal,* Emerson said, an animal
housed in the pleasure and sorrow of flesh.
We should continue to discover those words
that will transform the only world
we have, to praise the movement of words
toward delicate and shifting fields of light.

Without Even the Thought of a Net

—George Looney

Maybe language can redeem the difficult,
broken landscapes we live in,
but for whom? Redemption for beavers
is just another swamp for us.
When they dam up creeks, somewhere else
all that depended on the flow of water
suffers and has to move on. If Emerson
was right, the bestiary that forms our bodies
is a delicate balancing act. Even
how we speak of it is a thin wire,
and we could just be one of those
trained monkeys or bears that hold
the wire burning and bloody between toes
and behave in ways no monkey or bear
would call dignified for the amusement
of broken people who come to watch
such sad sideshows as we are. Ancient stories
are riddled with these animals that speak
and move about as people. In those tales,
the high wires of their hearts are precarious,
without even the thought of a net.
And the applause of the crowd
doesn't keep any of us from the sad dirt
that passes for a floor, or comfort us
alone in the air. More often than not,
what we move toward turns out not to be

34

a field, but the stagnant water
of some foul swamp reflecting the tortured,
fraudulent light of an indifferent moon.
Still, deer sometimes come to the edge
of swamps. And it is for the possibility
of such grace that we hold the wire
with what flesh and words we have left.
Even angels fall to the earth. Perhaps
we're doomed to fall with whatever grace
we can muster, and form a language
that can name what we would love. Hold on,
friend, and fall with the grace of your words.
Angels have nothing on us, it turns out,
this a dispatch from the asylum,
where one of the madnesses is how the angels,
who torture us, come sometimes in the night
and whisper gentle words which find
wounds in our flesh to lie down in
and go to rot. Once an angel knelt outside
my door and asked me not to punish her
by crying out and writhing in the chains.
Don't punish me, she whispered
through the door. *It's not my fault.* Later,
she came back. I must have been whimpering.
There's nothing I can do about it, she said,
before moving off down the hall
toward a life she lives beyond this asylum.
A life in which someone is happy.
I've heard rumors of such places. Once,
I believed such places existed.

Such faith doesn't last long in this asylum.
Is belief in such places a madness,
or grace? Or both? Does it matter?
Let's choose to believe. The only way to get there
is to believe it into existence and go.

From Darkness

–Douglas Smith

The gospel of despair continues,
but my son saves me
from darkness. Robert Hayden
would certainly understand:
What did I know, what did I know
of love's austere and lonely
offices? Please let me know
if I can help you
move through your own offices.

Gargoyles Along the Rib Cage

—George Looney

David Bottoms speaks of *those dwarfed*
transfiguring angels who have *mercy*
enough to consume us all and give us wings.
Angels who carry suffering with them
like a kind of dust, angels who *are* suffering,
can only change us into themselves.
(As Rilke said, we consume the world
and change it *endlessly, oh endlessly,*
into ourselves.) After enough encounters
with angels, we're forced to accept
all we can have of angels in our lives
is the dust that drifts over us
off their perfect bodies, the sorrow
that builds flying buttresses
around our hearts and places gargoyles
(those stone icons of suffering
that have no language to speak their lives
out of the stone they're made of)
along the rib cage, turned in toward
the red sky they believe is paradise.
It is not. It is time to take a hammer to
the stone bodies perched in that red light
and release what is inside. I have
raised the hammer. The stone
trembles. My arm is coming down.

Our Love of This

   –Douglas Smith

When we speak of paradise, we must speak
of the sacred possibility of love.
The opposite of love is not hate but indifference,
Elie Wiesel said. We have both
discovered the terrible truth of that sentence,
but we must not allow indifference
to shatter tenderness and passion and faith.
We must remember what William Kittredge said
in *Hole in the Sky: If we want to be happy*
at all, I think, we have to acknowledge
that the circumstances which encourage us
in our love of this existence are essential.
We are part of what is sacred. That is
our main defense against craziness,
our solace, the source of our best politics,
and our only chance at paradise. Please
know your presence in my life
encourages me to believe in
a certain form of paradise here
in the broken world, which is a blessing.

A Whisper of Missing Water

—George Looney

Who are we to speak of paradise, or love?
Who are we to look into the sky
and claim anything is sacred? To say
angels *don't* move among us, touching us
when we're most vulnerable
and telling each other the dreams
they take without our missing them?
What are dreams that we should miss them?
And who are we to say any life is broken,
or healed? Angels are a confusion
of touch, and they whisper to the sky
as though light had a choice. Paradise,
one of them whispers in the cold
shell of my ear, is filled with the illusion
of water, but there is no water. Paradise
is empty, a jig played in the style
of a dirge. It's what informs the whispers
of those of us formed of mud
who remember its suffering in our marrow.
Who are we to hum the tunes
of pleasure or suffering to one another?
The answer is, of course, we are
the ones whose bodies score the music
no instrument can play. And if we are
to believe in paradise, we must
let the angels pass through us and still

believe in touch, in the fluid tune
of a dirge that follows us all our lives.
We must love the following, love
the dirge. My friend, play the dirge,
if you must, and you must,
on an instrument whose music is
a whisper of missing water. Dance
to the song your playing forms.
The music you dance to is a touch
that heals all broken flesh. Be healed
in the dance, in the act of healing.
And send back whatever whispers
you steal from the angels. Remember,
healing loves company. And only
in the company of angels can we be healed.

No Guards

–Douglas Smith

Sometimes I believe the world
has become a small cold cell
in an immense penal colony,
but then my remarkable son
enters the room, and I am saved:
the windows are open,
and there are no bars; the gates
are unlocked, and there
are no guards. I wrestle against
despair, which is one way
of not seeing the world entire.
I wrestle because I desire another
world, and I want you to do the same.

The Light Such Thought Should Be

—George Looney

What comfort is there in the jealousy of angels?
Even if they hover so close to us
they drift in and out of our bodies,
we can't touch them. And it's through touch
forgiveness comes to us. Remember this.
It's through touch pain leaves us, our sorrow
transfigured. The indifference of angels
comes from the fact they can't touch the world.
Or is it possible the longing to touch
is touch itself? Remember the angels
in Wim Wenders' film? One so longs
to rid himself of his distance from the world
of touch he's able to give up eternity.
As though touch were salvation. Even now
I believe it is. But what has he given up?
For us, without passion, eternity
is a dark torture in which the thought of light
is only a ruse, and not the light
such thought should be, and is, with passion.
Even if the light is just the glow
left behind by the passing through our flesh
of an angel. What are we ever left?
Ourselves? Can that be enough? Listen
for angels as they move through you.
For though Rilke may have been right
that the angels won't hear us if we cry out,

we need to hear them. Only by caring
do we remain human and so of interest
to the angels. Remember this.
Don't be afraid to listen and hear
whatever angels you might hear in listening.

The Broken World We Live In

–Douglas Smith

We must remember the anguish of darkness
in order to shape our desire for light.
If we do not remember that anguish,
then we cannot tell the stories that make us
human. We must speak, then,
of a million figures moving through
a landscape of ash and blood. We must speak of
trains gliding across empty fields
toward madness. We must speak of flesh
stained with numbers and bodies rising into air.
We must move through the gates
of Auschwitz and Dachau and Treblinka
and Belsen. We do not want to enter that world,
but we must, for there is a voice rising
from the silence. *Listen,* the voice tells us again
and again. *We were here.* We listen to
that voice, and we are amazed at the broken world
we live in. We are amazed at the mystery
of what it means to be human.
We close our eyes and remember
what the messengers said to Job:
and I only am escaped alone to tell thee.
We have seen darkness, and now
we can consider the possibility of light.

The Grace of Statues

–George Looney

In the asylum, it's not the broken world we live in
that amazes us, but the broken world
that lives in us. How our screams
sink continents in a world we imagine,
instead of our hearts, in our chests.
No matter how much history moves through
our bodies like burning rivers
that carve charred and desperate channels,
no matter what is burned and drifts the air
like ash we could love, our anguish
remains in the care of indifferent angels
who come in our pain and our grief
and stare at us with the grace of statues,
the compassion of oblivion. And what good
is enduring, when it just makes possible
more pain? The number I would speak of
stains flesh differently than the blue numbers
of the holocaust. The number
I would place against the pull of history
is the number of days I have felt
close to an angel, which is a finite number.
Angels don't understand this. They don't
understand limits, or death. It's not
something they think of. For them,
it's a vague memory. Not something
to feel. Remember, we are human.

46

And remember that, because we are,
every relationship is terminal. Remember
this is both a burden and a joy
that denies indifference. That can heal
landscapes, raise continents. Hold to that.
It may be all that separates us
from the vast indifference of angels,
the only thing that makes light possible.

To the Brink of Fear

–Douglas Smith

When we walk into the shifting landscape of passion,
we always walk into the possibility of pain.
We know that, and still we walk, for we are thirsty.
Paul Zweig certainly walked into that same landscape:
Thirst made me a man. If a man is someone
who drinks pain, and is still thirsty. I have been
thirsty for a long time, but something remarkable
has happened to me: someone has carried passion
and grace into my life, and I am once again
alive and amazed. *I have enjoyed a perfect exhilaration,*
Emerson said. *I am glad to the brink of fear.*
Exhilaration always contains an edge of fear,
a shiver of darkness, and still we walk. I have
certainly known fear and darkness in my life,
and I can certainly imagine your recent pain,
but I hope you will continue to walk into
that necessary landscape. *The bird of sympathy*
howled in my sleep, Zweig wrote. I believe
I understand this beautiful and terrifying sentence.
Consider this one bird howling at another.

Open Your Mouth to the Sky

—George Looney

A body, Larry Levis wrote, *wants to be held,*
& held, & what/Can you do about that?
What indeed? The only thing we can do
is hope to find someone to hold and be held by.
I'm glad you've found someone. Here,
in the cool nights of northern Ohio, the birds
are howling in my sleep. I don't know
if they're birds of sympathy, or cruelty.
It's terrifying how much the two sound alike.
And how the howls can change from one night
to the next. Maybe what howls in the wind
of Ohio are not birds, but those terrible angels
we've spoken about and spoken to. Maybe
it's not my sleep they howl in, but my waking.
Sometimes the howls come from close by,
other times from distances I have
no way to measure with any accuracy.
And sometimes the howls are inside me.
This is the first day of spring. Soon,
Christ will once again be sacrificed, made sacred.
Once again, he'll cry down from the cross,
speaking for us all, *I thirst.* This sad and sore spring,
he speaks for me all too well, my landscape
the mountain named for the skull. And pain
blooms, flowers that bleed and sing slow hymns
all night. Dark and sad hymns I hear

under the howls. There is little grace in this
wasteland. It's good to get dispatches
from a place where grace is less elusive.
The dry soil I walk on (and yes, I'm still walking,
limping as best I can) has been betrayed
by water. Even the clouds on the horizon
won't burst here. Dance in the rain for us both.
And open your mouth to the sky
that fills with wings and water. Drink, my friend.
Hold to your grace. I hope it holds you
the way all bodies need to be held. And held.
Or howl, asleep or awake, knowing
no angel will hear us. Only birds. All the birds.

A Note From the Author

After Douglas and I graduated from Bowling Green State University with our MFA degrees, his in fiction and mine in poetry, we never lived in the same city again. We visited one another when we could, met at AWP Conferences when both of us could get funding from the educational institutions we were working at to attend, and we spent time over two different summers in Austin, Texas researching the William Goyen special issue of *Mid-American Review*. And we sent letters back and forth. Yes, through the US mail. These poems started out as those letters. At some point we decided to work with a particular series of those letters, to hone them into poems, and to create this chapbook of corresponding poems. Sadly, Douglas did not live to see it in print. But I'm glad that these poems of his (with mine) have now been published, so that a little more of Douglas' wonderful writing is available to be read.

—George Looney

Douglas Smith

Douglas Smith was born in San Juan, Puerto Rico in 1959. When he died unexpectedly in 2018, he was working at Guilford College in his native North Carolina. Before his death, he had published a chapbook of microfictions, *Judgments*, and had had poems in such journals as *The Gettysburg Review, The American Journal of Poetry, Hayden's Ferry Review, Cimarron Review, Lake Effect, Roanoke Review, The South Carolina Review,* and *Mid-American Review*. A posthumous collection, *The Ceremony of Opening the Mouth: The Poetry and Prose of Douglas Smith,* is forthcoming from Hermit Feathers Press.

George Looney

George Looney's books include the forthcoming *The Visibility of Things Long Submerged*, winner of the BOA Editions Short Fiction Award, *Ode to the Earth in Translation, The Worst May Be Over,* which won the Elixir Press Fiction Award, *The Itinerate Circus: New and Selected Poems 1995-2020,* the Red Mountain Press Poetry Award-winning *What Light Becomes: The Turner Variations,* and the novel *Report from a Place of Burning* which was co-winner of The Leapfrog Press Fiction Award. He is the founder of the BFA in Creative Writing Program at Penn State Erie, editor-in-chief of the international literary journal *Lake Effect,* translation editor of *Mid-American Review,* and co-founder of the original Chautauqua Writers' Festival.